THE SECOND BOOK O

Word games, riddles, codes and puzzles to stump, perplex, flummox, mystify and outwit you!

Starring all your friends from *Jigsaw*.

THE SECOND BOOK OF
JIGSAW PUZZLES

CLIVE DOIG
Illustrated by Malcolm Bird

KNIGHT/BBC

©British Broadcasting Corporation 1981
*First published by Knight Books/ British
Broadcasting Corporation 1981*

British Library C.I.P.

Doig, Clive

 The second book of jigsaw puzzles
 (Knight books)
 1. Word games
 I. Title
 793.73   GV1507.W8

 ISBN 0 340 27745 9
    (0 563 20016 2 BBC)

---

*This book is sold subject to the condition that
it shall not, by way of trade or otherwise, be
lent, re-sold, hired out or otherwise circulated
without the publisher's prior consent in any
form of binding or cover other than that in
which this is published and without a similar
condition including this condition being
imposed on the subsequent purchaser.*

*Filmset by ©ollins, Glasgow
Printed and bound in Great Britain for
Hodder and Stoughton Paperbacks, a
division of Hodder and Stoughton Ltd,
Mill Road, Dunton Green, Sevenoaks, Kent
(Editorial Office: 47 Bedford Square,
London WC1 3DP) and the
British Broadcasting Corporation,
35 Marylebone High Street, London W1M 4AA
by Richard Clay (The Chaucer Press), Ltd.,
Bungay, Suffolk*

Here are hundreds more jigwords, jigsaws, mazes and puzzles to baffle you, just like the ones in my programme. I hope you find them fun to do.

They will certainly 'give someone something to think about'.

Pterry's stopped speaking in proverbs, but he still says very pompous things and he likes to speak in IDIOMS. By the way IDIOMS is one of the Jigwords in the book.

I expect you will 'catch someone out' with that.

Yes, Pterry, I expect we will.

Anyway, all the puzzles in my book are based on my popular puzzle programme shown on BBC 1, with Pterry, the nearly-extinct Pteranodon; Biggum, the sixty-foot Scottish giant and all the others who appear – the O-men, Cid Sleuth and of course Adrian Hedley and Janet Ellis – and, most important, Clive Doig, the producer of the show.

What is a Jigword?

It's a six-letter word and you have to guess it. There are over a hundred Jigwords in this book (the answers are at the back) and each one can be guessed by clues to the letters like this:

1. (First letter) The sound a snake makes (*sss*).

2. (Second letter) A letter which is is the same upside down (*I*).

3. (Third letter) Two ens make an (*m*).

4. (Fourth letter) Vegetable or sweet flower (*p*).

5. (Fifth letter) You'll find it in laugh and also in smile (*l*).

6. (Sixth letter) The fifth letter of the alphabet (*e*).

Fill the answer in the blank spaces of the Jigword box.

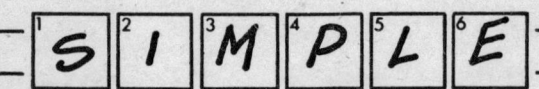

That was SIMPLE wasn't it?

'Och! Aye, even I could do that, hoots, man.'

Well done, Biggum!

We start off with easy ones and get more difficult later on.

If you want even more difficult Jigwords there's also my 'Third Book of Puzzles' for you to try.

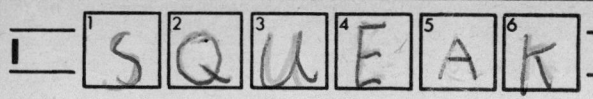

Off we go...
Here's the first Jigword. See if you can do it.

1. The first letter of the first Jigword is the first letter in all these clothes.

2. This may be of some help to the second letter.

3. The third letter is in all these animals.

4. The fourth letter is the first initial of these famous people.

_ _ _ _ _ _ Presley, _ _ _ _ _ _ John, _ _ _ _ _ Everage, _ _ _ _ _ _ _ Rantzen.

5. This musical note  is the fifth letter.

6. The last letter is also the last letter missing from all these words –

IN___, DUC___, SHAR___ and SQUEA___

 Have you got it?

2 — P O W D E R

1. The missing letter in these abbreviations —
?.M., P.?.S., ?.T.O., R.S.V.?.

___

2. Bangle, Quoit, Hoop, Tyre, Ring, Halo, Torus.
Those things might give you a clue to this letter.

___

3. An M upside down.

___

4. It is in  but not

It is in but not

___

5. It ends all these edible things YUM! YUM!

___

6. It sounds like a cry of anguish.

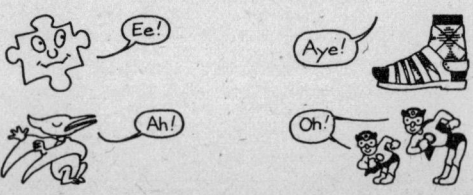

BIGGUM'S JIGSAW PUZZLE NO. 1

Biggum Plays Tennis

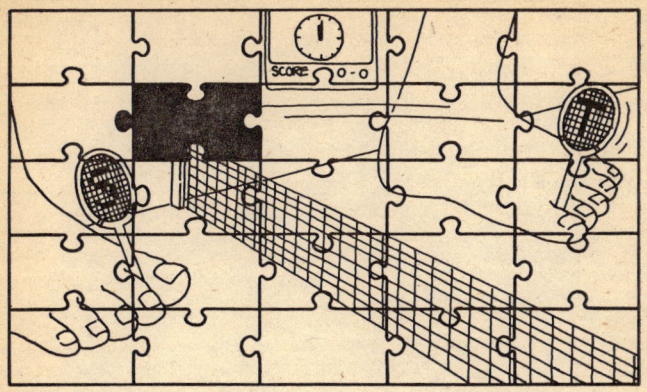

Find the ball!

Which of the jigsaw pieces below fits Biggum's Jigsaw?

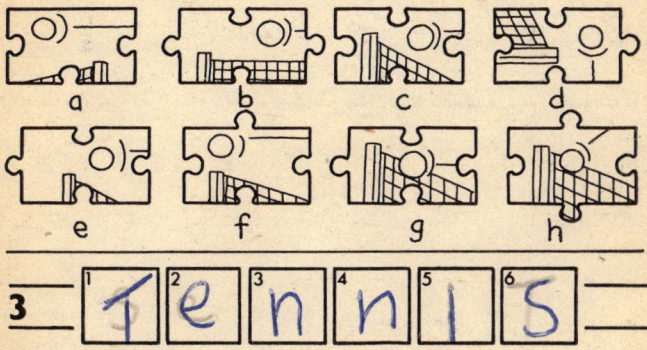

| 3 | ¹T | ²e | ³n | ⁴n | ⁵ı | ⁶S |

1. The letter on Biggum's left hand racket.
2. The answer to the puzzle above.
3. & 4. The time on the clock minus the score.
5. How many people are playing tennis in the drawing?
6. The letter on Biggum's right-hand racket.

4. W I Z A R D

1. This letter looks like two other letters joined together.

2. 👁

3. What letter is missing twice from this strange word: _IG _AG ... it looks like it too!

4. Aquariums are full of angel fish. ◁ ◁ ◁

5. Finish off these words:
MOO__ DOO__ FLOO__ SPOO__
INDOO__ POO__
... but be careful the O-men don't hear you (see page 26).

6. There's a river in Cheshire called this letter.

5. V A N I S H

1. Five on this clock ...

2. Which is the only vowel that does not occur in any number from one to ninety-nine?

3. A 'Z' turned over.

4. This letter is in FINGER but not in THUMB
it is in CHIN but not in CHEEK
and it is in WRIST but not in HAND.

5. If Sixty-six Sheep were in a field and one died, how many would be left?
Well, it depends how you say 'Sixty Sick Sheep.'
ANSWERS: Sixty-five Sheep or fifty-nine Sick Sheep!

6. What a hitch hiker has to begin with, apart from a thumb.

Did you know you can always get through a maze by touching one wall on one side continuously.
Try it with this simple maze, follow either the left- or right-hand wall.

6 _ | | R | U | B | B | Y | _

Now it gets a little more difficult...
What is missing?

1. Air on a... string.

2. ... for mo (see page 50).

3. Make a... turn.

4. Flight of the bumble...

5. To... or not to...

6. ...do people ask..., when they want to know something?

7 _ | P | I | M | P | L | E | _

1. More common in pepper than in salt.

2. This letter is also a word.

3. The sound of humming.

4. It would look like this b upside down in a mirror.

5. This letter looks a bit like a book end, the one on the right-hand end!

6. The most common letter in the English language.

8. A N G E L A

Find the missing letter in each of the names and you will spell another name.

1. ...GATHA

2. A...ABEL

3. IN...RID

4. PHO...BE

5. MYRT...E

6. JOANN...

9. S T D N E Y

This time one letter has been changed in each of the names below. Find out which one and you will get another name.

1. BADIL

2. PAN

3. GOFFREY

4. SOEL

5. MYRVYN

6. ROM

ABCDEFGHIJKLMNOPQRSTUVWXYZ
CODES, CIPHERS AND SECRET WRITING
The simplest form of code is where you substitute every individual letter in a message for *either*
a) another letter, *or*
b) a number, *or*
c) a different symbol.

In any substitution code you must have a pattern or key of what you, the sender, should do to encode the message and what the receiver should do to decode it. For instance, if all the letters are substituted by the next letter in the alphabet, then a message like:
MEET ME AT NOON would read:
NFFU NF BU OPPO

The pattern here is 'Shift + 1'. To decode it you would have to go back one letter in the alphabet.

A B C D E F G H I J K L M N O P Q R S T U V W X Y Z
B C D E F G H I J K L M N O P Q R S T U V W X Y Z A

Similarly a substitution 'Shift + 3' (i.e. shift along three letters in the alphabet) would turn SEE YOU AT SIX into VHH BRX DW VLA

A B C D E F G H I J K L M N O P Q R S T U V W X Y Z
D E F G H I J K L M N O P Q R S T U V W X Y Z A B C

In substitution code 'Shift + 7' the message:
THE KEY IS UNDER THE MAT reads MAX DXR BL NGWXK MAX FTM

Of course, if the substitution was + 13 (or − 13, it is the same) then as well as A being substituted by N, N would also be substituted by A; and so on:
B for O and O for B etc.
EAT THE RING = RNG GUR EVAT

What is the Jigword here?

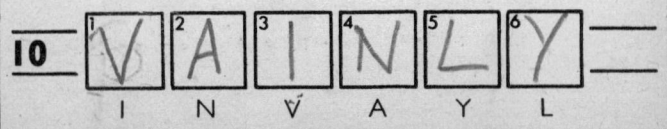

10 | V | A | I | N | L | Y |
| I | N | V | A | Y | L |

To help you here is the full code 'Shift + 13'

A B C D E F G H I J K L M
N O P Q R S T U V W X Y Z

Another double substitution could be

A B C D E F G H I J K L M
Z Y X W V U T S R Q P O N

Here is a Jigword in this 'reverse double'

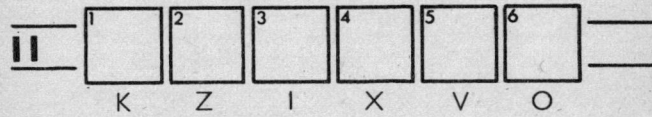

K Z I X V O

If you have the alphabet written out in front of you it is quite easy to crack a code written with regular substitutions which shift up and down the alphabet. To make a code more difficult you could use a keyword only known to you and the receiver, a word like PTERODACTYL for instance. Write out the keyword, and write the rest of the alphabet underneath. Now you have your own substitution code in which you substitute the top letter for the bottom letter and vice versa. (Note that the second T in Pterodactyl is missed out because it has already been used.)

P T E R O D A C Y L B F G
H I J K M N Q S U V W X Z

Here is a message in 'Pterodactyl' code sent by Pterry to Jigg:

HIJKKU TC LJKU WKQTDU QDN SVJLJK

Jigg's reply:    HIJKKU TC Q WTZPJQN!

Of course a thirteen-letter word with all different letters in it would be a far better keyword. The word *Consumptively* has thirteen different letters in it, although it is not a very nice word, it makes a super keyword:

CONSUMPTIVELY
ABDFGHJKQRWXZ

Can you work out what the Jigword is using that code?

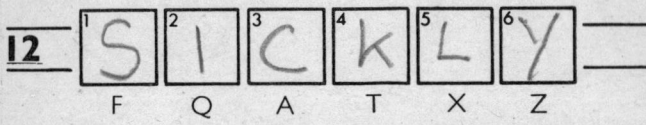

As well as substituting letters for other letters or numbers you could also jumble up your message by changing the order of the letters, this is called a 'Transposition' code. The message below will be put into code in this way:

JIGSAW VIEWERS ARE VERY INTELLIGENT

First write it backwards:

TNEGILLETNI YREV ERA SREWEIV WASGIJ

Then take every second letter in the message and write them all down in a long string:

NGLENRVRSEEVAGJTEILTYEEARWIWSI

Now substitute letters using the 'consumptively' code:

DUXWDVRVFWWRCUPKWQXKZWWCVEQEFQ

Finally use a brand new 'symbol' code and split up the message into groups of five:

⊐⏃⋖⋁⏌ ⋗⋲⊏⋁⏀ ⋁⋂⋌⋁⊐ ⊔⋁⋀⋖⊔ ⋗⋁⋁⋌⋗ ⊓⋂⊐⊏⋂

The message is now in 'PIGPEN' code (see page 78). Or you could use a foreign alphabet to further confuse (see page 30 for some funny alphabets).

Each of these faces has been made out of a name. Can you find out who is who?

So, who is this?

| 13 | ¹E | ²V | ³E | ⁴L | ⁵Y | ⁶N |

14 | M | I | R | R | O | R |

NUMBERS

1. 3 ... this is the letter turned through 90°.

2. A very singular letter, this one.

3. The second person plural of the verb 'to be'.

4. It is in 3 and 4 but not in 5.

5. $6+1-2-5=$.

6. 2 of these in a circle equals D.

15 | P | I | G | S | T | Y |

1. The only letter that can finish these words
AL____ AM____ AS____.

2. The middle letter of the following:
PIN, KNIFE, WHITE, PAINT.

3. The seventh letter of the alphabet.

4. The letter that fits between these two words to make a word:
MY____ELF.

5. The letter that goes at both ends of all these words:
____O____, ____A____, ____I____, ____U____, ____OO____.

6. A questioning letter?

| **16** | E | I | G | H | T | Y |

The first letters of each of these pictures:

1. egg

2. INK

3. GUN

4. hat

5. toe

6. Yak

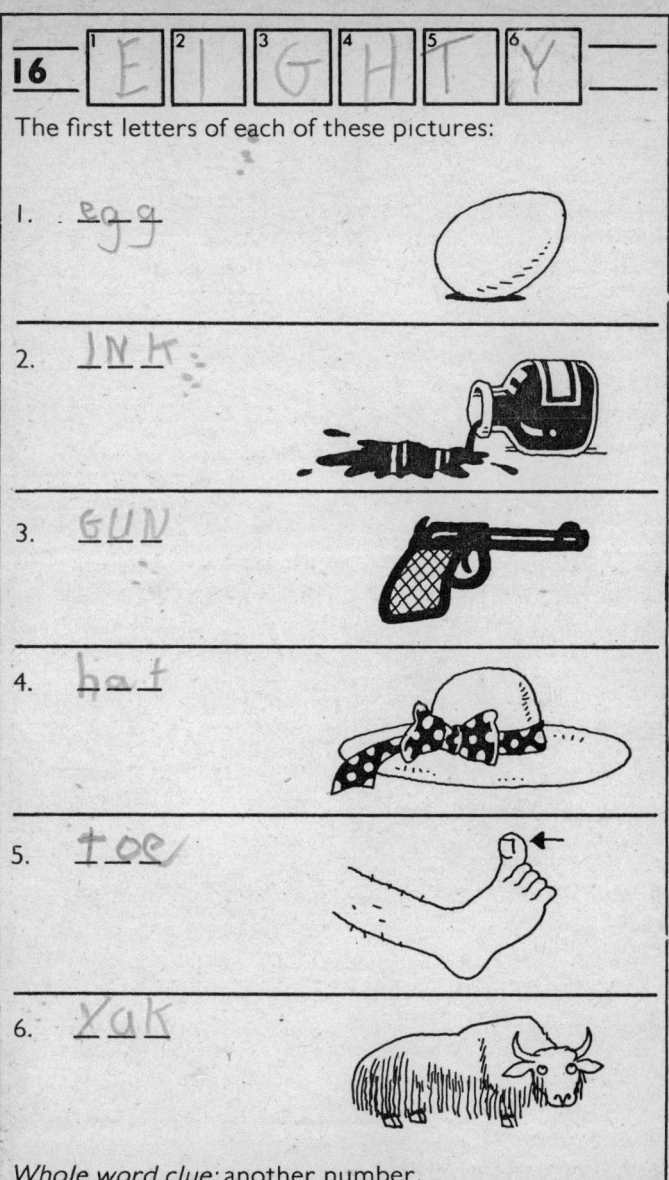

Whole word clue: another number.

FISHING MAZE

Adrian, Pterry, Janet, the O-men, Jigg and Biggum have gone fishing. Can you follow their fishing lines and see what each has caught?

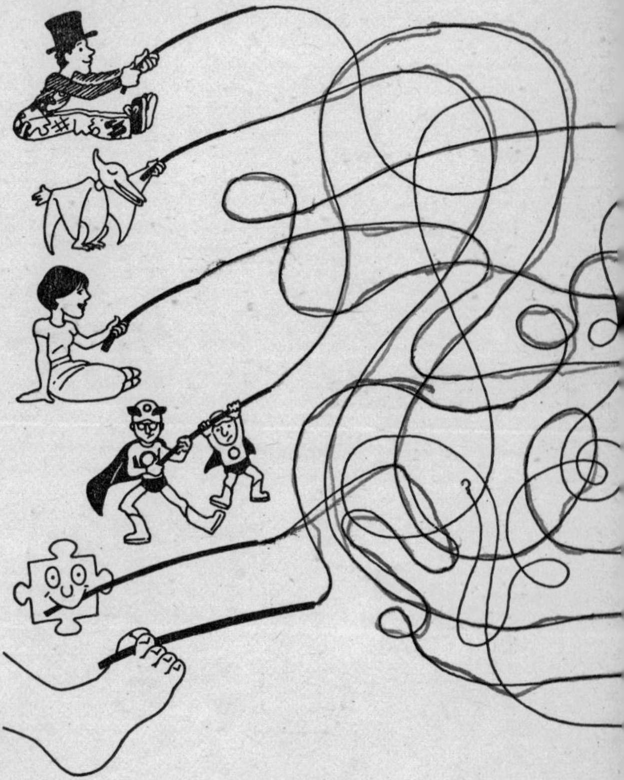

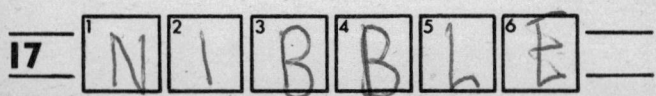

17

1	2	3	4	5	6
N	I	B	B	L	E

If you take the first letters of whatever they have each caught you will get the Jigword.

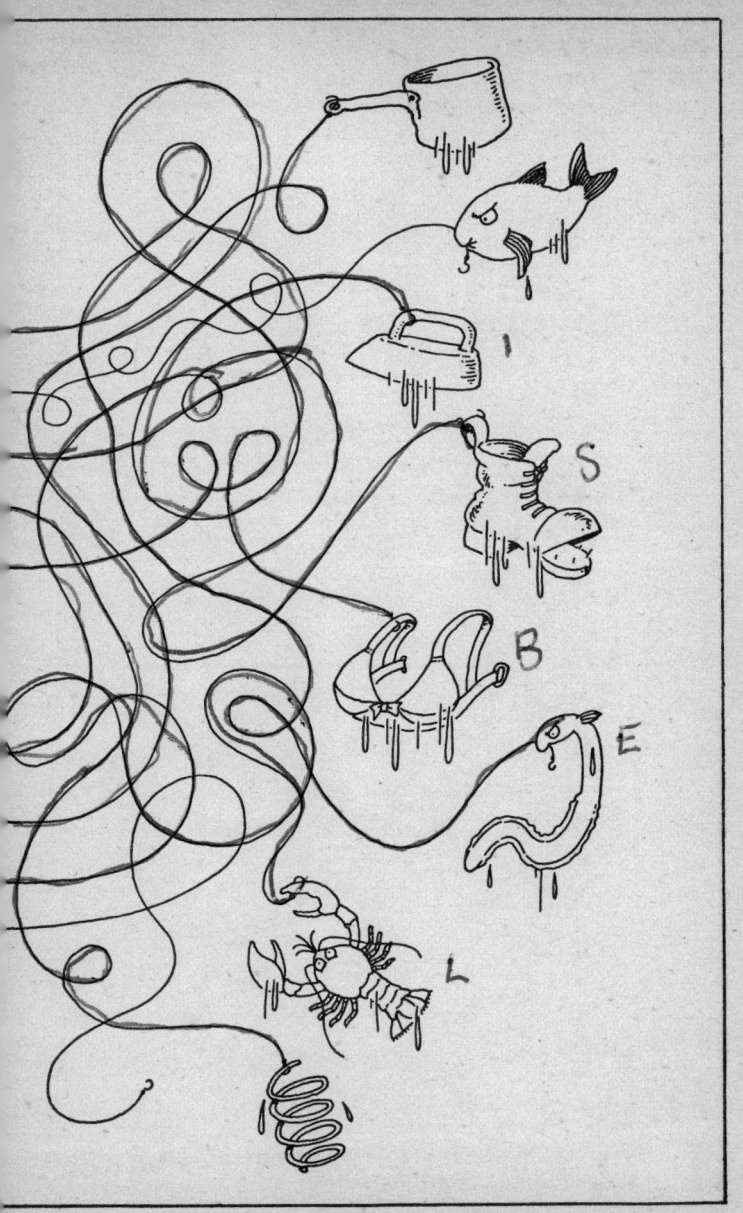

18 | b | e | a | u | t | y |

First letters again:

1. bell

2. eagle

3. apple

4. umbrella

5. tree

6. yahyt

19 | C | o | r | s | e | t |

Each of the answers to the clues contains a double letter, write them down and get the Jigword.

1. Another word for football. soccer
2. The part of a plant under the ground. root
3. A word of apology. sorry
4. The lowest voice. bass
5. An insect that stings. bee
6. Something else that stings. nettle

20 | o | x | y | g | e | n |

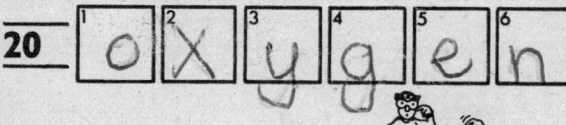

1. The roundest letter of all.

2. A very cross letter.

3. The last letter of every day.

4. The twentieth letter from the end of the alphabet.

5. The letter seen on a Spanish car.

6. This letter occurs twice in NONE
once in ONCE
and no times in TWICE.

Whole word clue: It is in the air, and in water, and you cannot have fire without it.

21 | b | o | t | t | o | m |

Use the double letter from each of these things:

1. ribben

2. foot

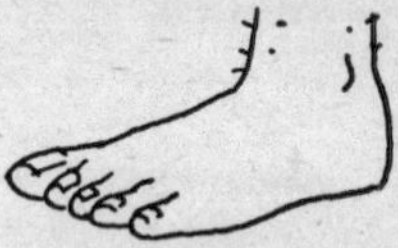

3. button

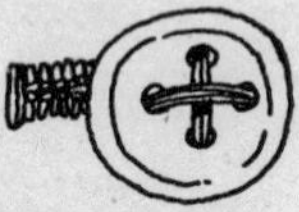

4. rattle

5. moon

6. dummy

I've got to get to the bottom of this.

22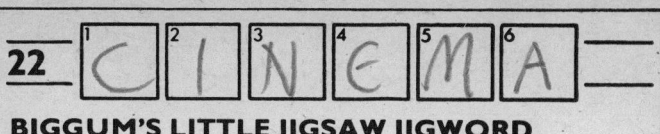

BIGGUM'S LITTLE JIGSAW JIGWORD
Re-arrange these six pieces of jigsaw so that they fit together and make a word.

23 — | C | A | S | t | l | e | —

A special Jigword from the O-men.

Remember the O-men appear whenever someone says six words with double 'O' in a row. This puzzle of theirs looks as if it could be pretty tricky:

1. Find the missing letter:

   _C_OOK _C_OOL _C_OOT _C_OOP _C_OON
   (only five words in a row there).

2. What goes in the middle of each of these words?
   B___N F___D R___T P___L CH___SE ST_A_GE
   (and it isn't OO).

3. Another missing letter starts all these:
   ___TOOL ___HAMPOO ___COOTER
   ___POON ___COOP ___HOE
   (thank goodness the last one wasn't _hoo).

4. The same letter fits in between the O's in all these words:
   MO_t_OR PHO_t_O O_t_OLOGY
   NO_t_ORIETY RIO_t_OUS CO_tt_ON.

5. In the following words one of the letters at either end has been substituted for the correct letter:

   FOOF MOOM POOP TOOT WOOW GUGG.

6. This letter has been changed for another one in all these words:

   FOOD ROOD LOOK BAA SLOOP CHOOSE
   (sorry about the 'baa' but you know why!)

You can say that again
You can say that again
*What again?

26

24

S	o	O	r	c	H
1	2	3	4	5	6

1. The most common letter in 'sausages'.

2. 100 in Roman numerals (see page 57).

3. Dinner –Dinner –Dinner –Dinner ? –Men.

4. Missing letter from these words
TEA____
TE____M
T____AM
____EAM

5. Half a circle.

6. Rugby posts.

25

m	u	F	F	A	n
1	2	3	4	5	6

1. This is the opposite of the third letter of Jigword No. 2.

2. The shape of a horseshoe.

3. & 4. A double letter missing from all these words:

CO__EE   TO__EE   PU__IN
CHA__INCH   GIRA__E   TRA__IC.

5. This letter is a word and this is how people from some other countries would say it in their language:

'JAG' 'JE' 'JEG' 'ICH' 'JA' 'IK' 'SAJA' 'WO.'

6. A noisy noise annoys an oyster. That's ENough!

Some letters fit together, interlocking with their own shapes — like these Ts.

26 | ¹U | ²N | ³J | ⁴U | ⁵S | ⁶T

You can make some letters fit into each other.
Can you read the word below from the six letters interlocked left to right.

27 S T I F L E

This is another word made up from interlocking letters.

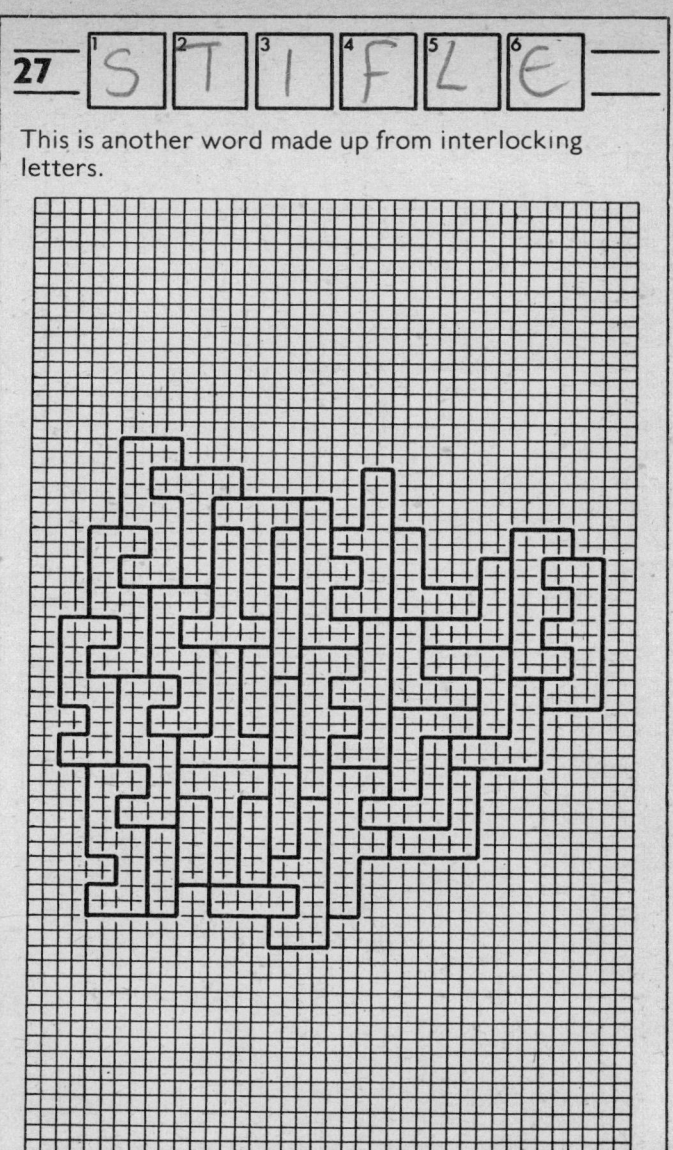

To work out how to interlock letters you need to first draw them out on graph paper. Here is the alphabet drawn in a square form with the help of graph paper. How many of these could interlock with each other without leaving any spaces?

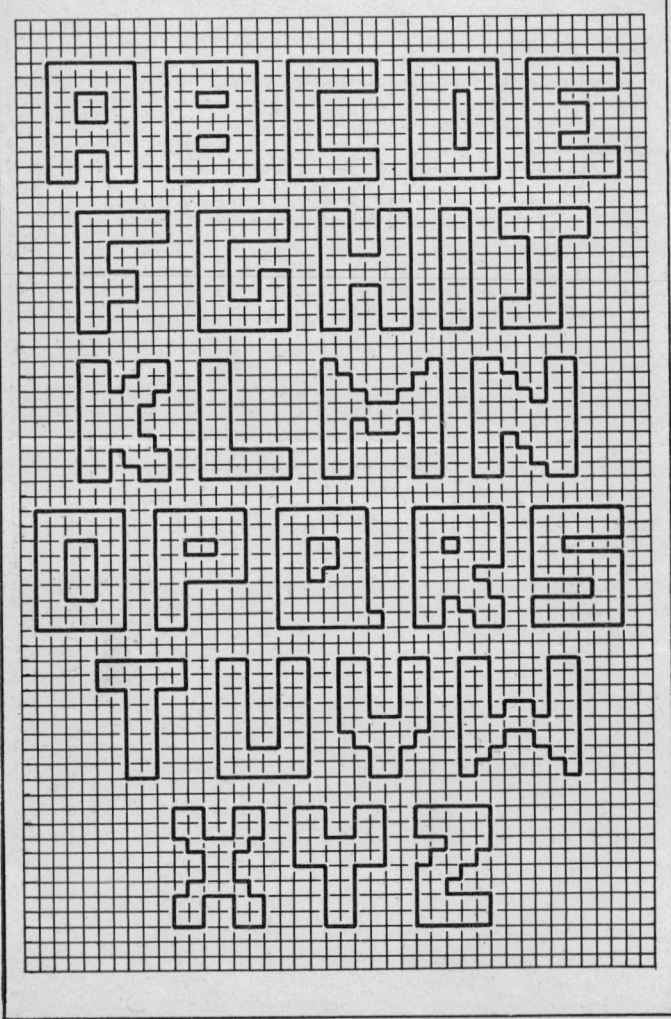

Here are some very strange letters:

A round alphabet

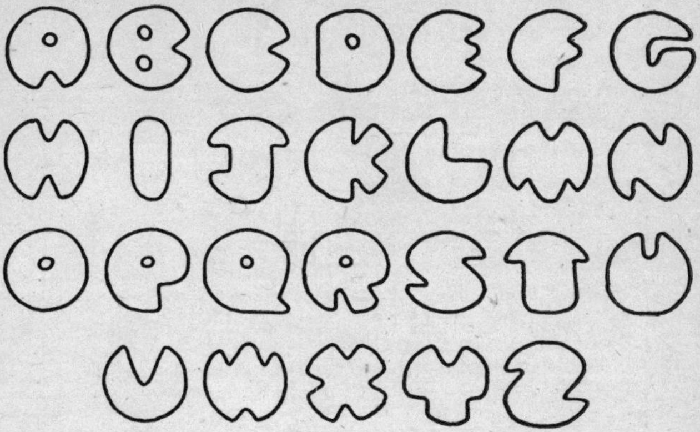

A B C D E F G
H I J K L M N
O P Q R S T U
V W X Y Z

A thin alphabet

A B C D E F G
H I J K L M N
O P Q R S T U
V W X Y Z

28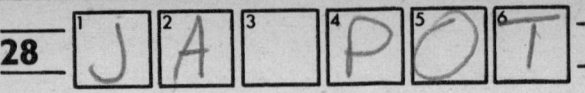

1. A bird.

2. An indefinite article.

3. A 'woolly mammoth' has three of them.

4. A vegetable.

5. $\frac{XII}{VII} - \pi =$

6. A drink.

29

SOUND-A-LIKES
If you work out the sounds of the answers below you will get the word.

1. To be in debt.

2. A tree often seen in graveyards.

3. On which to put a golf ball.

4. What you do with your eyes.

5. Present plural of the verb 'to be'.

6. A river at the end of Tintern Abbey.

SEASIDE

How many things beginning with S can you see here?

30 | W | A | T | E | R | Y |

There are at least twenty-five.
If you use the last letter of each of the things
numbered in order from 1 to 6 you will get another
Jigword.

THE O-MEN

What a beautiful picture of the O-men!
Now compare it with the picture opposite.
There have been a few changes...

There are over fifteen differences between this picture and the one opposite – what are they?

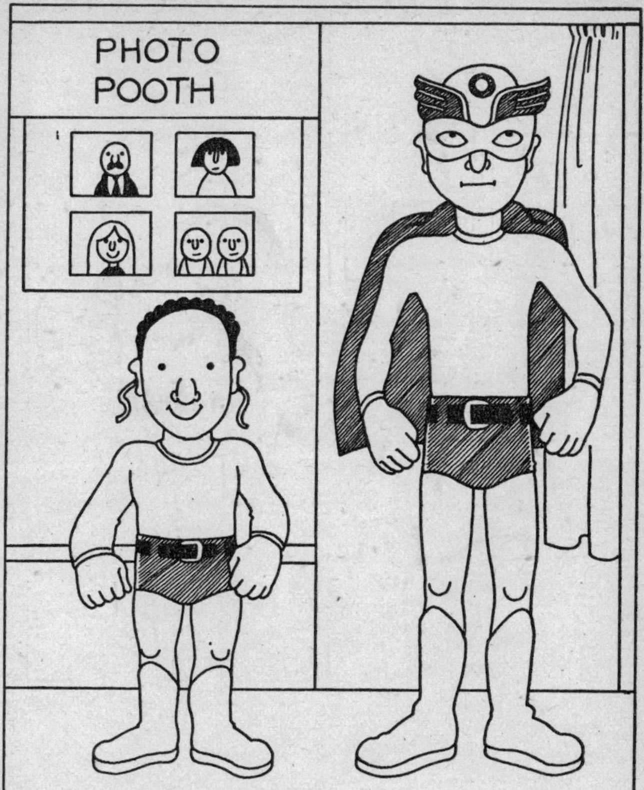

Six of the differences are things that were in the drawing opposite and are MISSING from this drawing. Write down the first letters of the missing things, jiggle them around and you can make up a Jigword.

31 | 1 | 2 | 3 | 4 | 5 | 6 |

Smile Mask Hair O, O, Cape

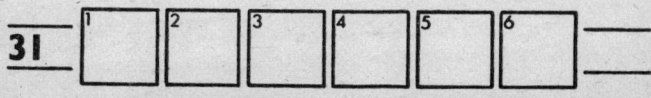

Two more Jigwords from the O-men.

32 | B | R | O | K | E | N |

Each of the answers to the clues has a double OO in it. Use the last letter of each answer.

1. A mistake — boob
2. Not rich — poor
3. Hair soap — shampoo
4. A chef — cook
5. A dog — poodle
6. Tropical rain storm — Monsoon

33 | C | H | O | R | A | L |

Use the second letter in these 'double O' answers.

1. Where children go to learn — school
2. To aim at goal — shoot
3. April or Gooseberry — Fool
4. Something to sweep up with — Broom
5. To make fun of — Lampoon
6. Opposite the ceiling — Floor

34 | R | E | C | K | O | n |

KNICKERBOCKER
Count off the letters of the word above, starting from the left according to the numbers below. For instance, the Seventh letter is R, write it down in the first box, and cross it off in KNICKERBOCKER. Now count through twelve more letters — if you get to the end of the word start at the beginning again.

1. 7
2. 12
3. 3
4. 8
5. 2
6. 5

You should have seven letters left out of 'Knickerbocker'. Cross out the middle letter and you've got Jigword 35.

35 | k | ~~n~~ | c | k | e | r |

I reckon that was pretty tricky.

I reckon it was pretty rude

JOIN THE DOTS
Join the dots from 1 to 76 and find out who this is.

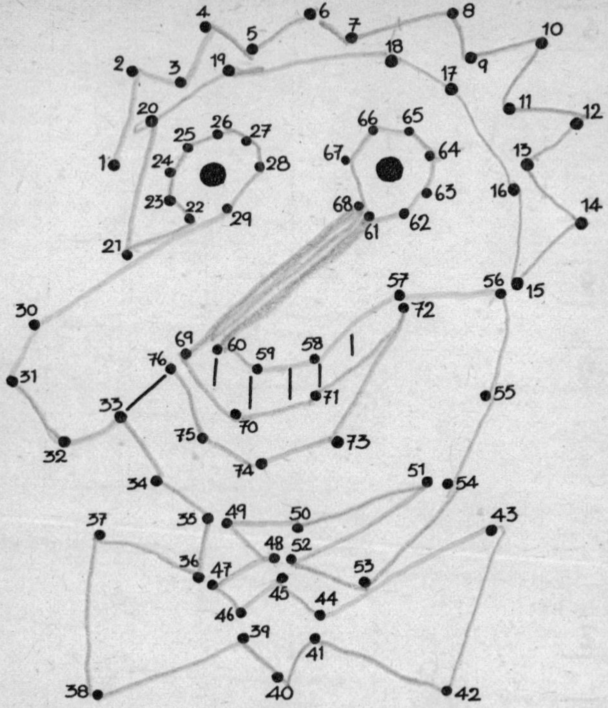

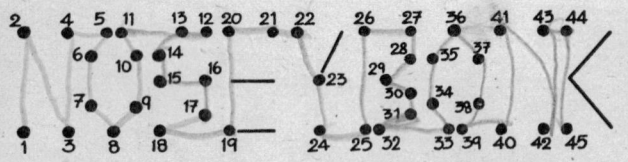

Well, do you know his name?

Each of the following Jigwords consists of two three-letter words (as CARPET is made up from CAR and PET), but they have got mixed up.
Can you sort them out and fit them into the word-square below.

KIDPUS – RUMTOE – KITHER – LAPNAP – RATTEN – TIPDOG

36	K	I	D	P	U	S
37	K	I	T	H	E	R
38	I	A	P	N	A	P
39				P		
40					E	
41						R

More mixed-up Jigwords

OFFEND – CATPIT – ADDACT – GOBICE – IMPLET – ARMKIN

42	C					
43		D				
44			B			
45				P		
46					C	
47						T

Another six mixed-up words
BEDSAW – OUTHEM – PEAWIT – NITPAN –
MAYSET – SEENUT

48. P E A N U T
49. M A Y H E M
50. N I T W I T
51. B E D P A N
52. S E E S A W
53. O U T S E T

And another lot...
OUTPOT – PIEWAY – MIDMAN – THEGET –
SEXBAN – RUNFIT

54. P I E M A N
55. _ U _ _ _ _
56. _ _ D _ _ _
57. _ _ _ B _ _
58. _ _ _ _ I _
59. _ _ _ _ _ T

SPOT THE DIFFERENCE

Here are two pictures of the same scene, one is the mirror image of the other.

Six drastic changes have happened in the mirror image. Can you spot them?

Here are the first letters of the things that have changed:

W<u>ALL</u>, G<u>ATE</u>, F<u>LAG</u>, S<u>moke</u>, S<u>UN</u>, F<u>IELD</u>

Write down the last letters of each and you will get the Jigword.

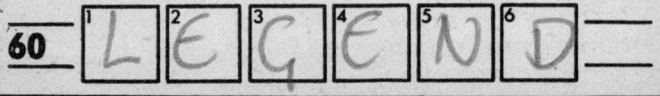

60 | ¹L | ²E | ³G | ⁴E | ⁵N | ⁶D

61 G A T H

Do you remember these amazing moments from my TV programme?

1. This letter ends every line of the rhyme but the last:
The orange orang-utang
Was hit by a boomerang,
Struck with a terrible twang
His howl round the forest rang,
Then off the branch the monkey sprang,
Hit the ground with a mighty clang,
Grabbed the boy with the boomerang,
Jabbered at him in apish slang,
Thumped his head with an awful bang,
The boy gulped back his hunger pang,
Regarded the empty overhang
And said 'Gee! What did I do that for?'

2. Adrian acquired an ancient Austrian apple and arrow auctioned at Andover.

3. '? for two and two for ?,
You for me and me for you.'
At ? one day Adrian sipped his ? out of the saucer and spilt it all over his ? -shirt.

4. This letter has been inserted where it shouldn't be and dropped where it should be:
A helephant eavily heats hat is hease,
Hunder humbracious humbrella trees.

5. Another poem, which this time contains every letter of the alphabet but one:
A Jack-in-the-box, with spring so strong,
Will quickly bring much joy,
But lazy boys find nothing wrong,
In having a clockwork toy.

6. Cid Sleuth's R-r-rest was R-r-rudely R-r-ruined by the R-r-rotten R-r-robber-r R-r-running off with his R-r-radio.

BIGGUM'S JIGSAW No. 3: TARGET

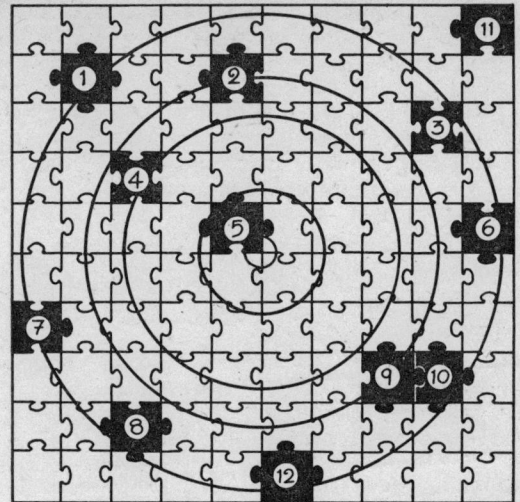

Can you find the twelve missing pieces and fit them into Biggum's 'Target' jigsaw.

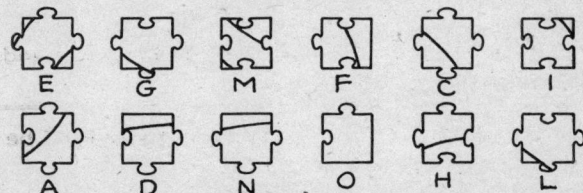

The letters under each piece will spell a Jigword if you fit them correctly into spaces 1–6

62

and also into spaces 7–12

63

A REBUS is a word which is represented in parts by pictures. For example, this is a rebus for a boy's name

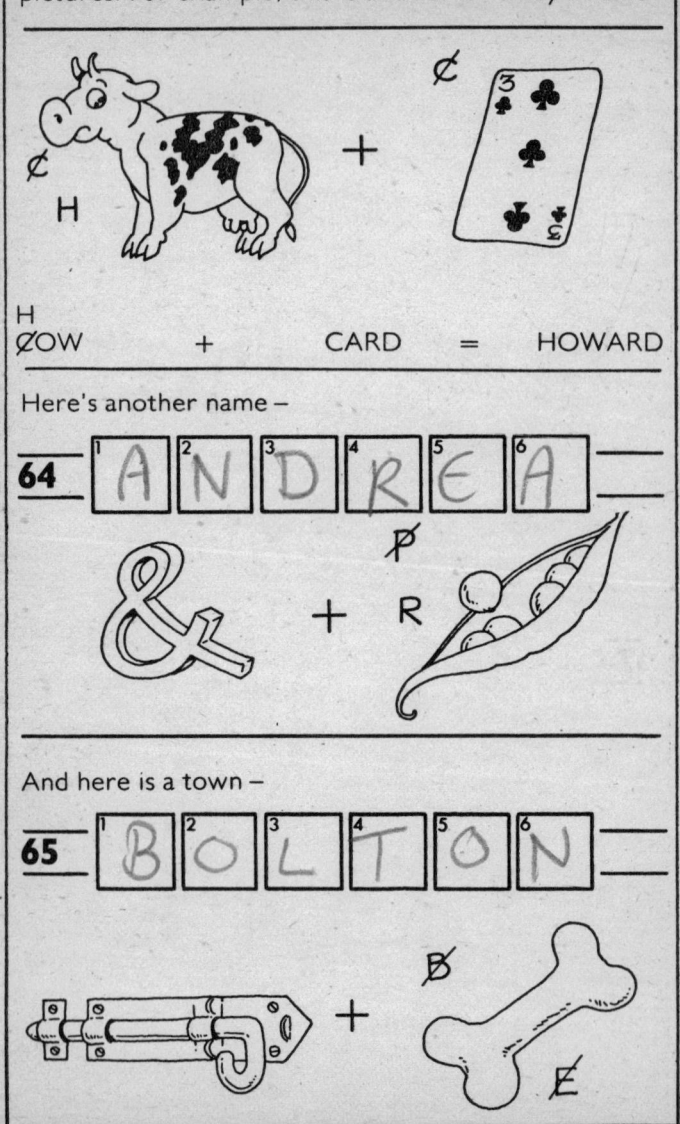

H
¢OW   +   CARD   =   HOWARD

Here's another name –

64 A N D R E A

And here is a town –

65 B O L T O N

TWO GIRLS' NAMES

66 F A N N I E

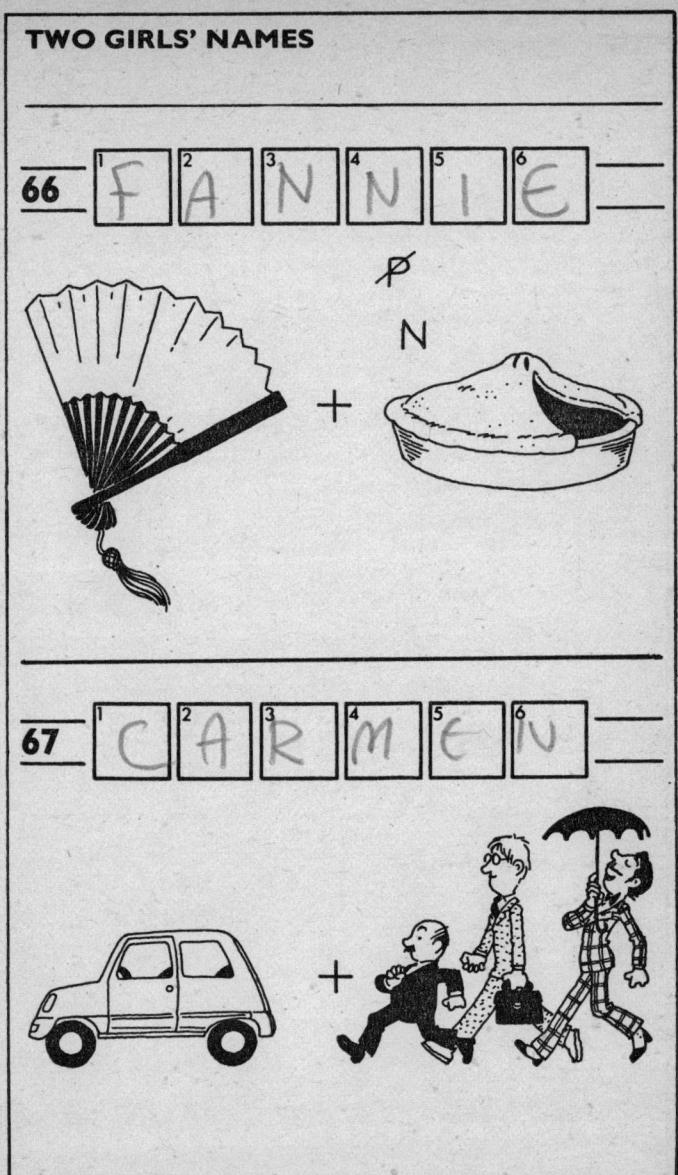

67 C A R M E N

OUR ALPHABET

Here are some examples of how some of the letters in our present-day alphabet, the Roman Alphabet, have developed over the last two or three thousand years. From the early pictographs or picture writing of Egypt and the Sinai, through Phoenician to the present day.

A	came from	Aleph	meaning	Ox
B	,,	Beth	,,	House
D	,,	Daleth	,,	Door
E	,,	He	,,	Window
G	,,	Gimel	,,	Camel
H	,,	Cheth	,,	Fence
I	,,	Yod	,,	Hand
K	,,	Kaph	,,	Palm of the hand
L	,,	Lamed	,,	Ox goad
M	,,	Mem	,,	Water
N	,,	Nun	,,	Fish
O	,,	'Ayin	,,	Eye
P	,,	Pe	,,	Mouth
Q	,,	Q'oph	,,	Knot
R	,,	Resh	,,	Head
S	,,	Shin	,,	Teeth
T	,,	Tau	,,	Mark
V	,,	Vau	,,	Hook
Z	,,	Zayin	,,	Weapons

Now you know the alphabet, see if you can work out these:

68 S H I E L D

69 B R O K E N

70 _ _ _ _ _ _

Mark Head Ox Water Mouth Teeth

ALPHABETS
Alphabets from other lands

GREEK	RUSSIAN	HEBREW	RUNES*
A = A alpha	А = A	ב = B	ᚠ = F
B = B beta	Б = B	ג = G	ᚢ = U
Γ = G gamma	В = V	ד = D	ᚦ = TH
Δ = D delta	Г = G	ה = H	ᚨ = A
E = E epsilon	Д = D	ו = W	ᚱ = R
Z = Z zeta	Е = YE	ז = Z	ᚲ = K
H = E eta	Ё = Yo	ח = H	ᚷ = G
Θ = Th theta	Ж = ZH	ט = T	ᚹ = W
I = I iota	З = Z	י = Y	ᚺ = H
K = K kappa	И = EE	כ = K	ᚾ = N
Λ = L lambda	Й = Y	ל = L	ᛁ = I
M = M mu	К = K	מ = M	ᛃ = J
N = N nu	Л = L	נ = N	ᛖ = E
Ξ = X xi	М = M	ס = S	ᛈ = P
O = O micron	Н = N	פ = P	ᛈ = P
Π = P. pi	О = O	צ = S	ᛉ = R
P = R rho	П = P	ק = Q	ᛋ = S
Σ = S sigma	Р = R	ר = R	ᛏ = T
T = T tau	С = S	ש = S	ᛒ = B
Υ = U upsilon	Т = T	ת = I	ᛗ = E
Φ = Ph phi	У = OO		ᛗ = M
X = KH chi	Ф = F		ᛚ = L
Ψ = PS psi	Х = KH		ᛝ = NG
Ω = Ō omega	Ц = TS		ᛟ = O
	Ч = CH		ᛞ = D
	Ш = SH		ᚾ = A
	Щ = SHCH		ᚫ = AE
	Ъ = —		ᛣ = Y
	Ы = i		ᛠ = EA
	Ь = y		ᛡ = IO
	Э = E		ᚻ = C
	Ю = Yoo		ᛤ = G
	Я = YA		

*Old Anglo-Saxon alphabet
(For another Runic alphabet see book 3)

These are all English Jigwords which have been written using the alphabets opposite:

71 | D | | | | | | ___

△ Y P I N Γ

72 | | | | | | | ___

Φ Ρ Ο Ζ Э Η

73 | | | | | | | ___

ᛉ ᛦ ᛉ | ᛉ ᛉ

74 | | | | | | | ___

ᚦ ᚱ ᛟ ᛯ

THE COCKNEY ALPHABET

Here is a reminder of a very strange alphabet:

A for 'Orses ('ay for 'orses)
B for Mutton (Beef or Mutton)
C for Miles (see for miles)
D for Ential (Differential)
E for Brick ('Eave a Brick)
F for Vessence (Effervescence)
G for Get It (Gee, forget it!)
H for Bless You (Aitsshfa! A sneeze)
I for The Engine (Ivor the Engine)
J for Oranges (Jaffa Oranges)
K for Restaurant (Cafe or Restaurant)
L for Leather ('Ell for Leather)
M for Sis (Emphasis)
N for Lope (Envelope)
O for The Garden Wall (Over the Garden Wall)
P for Relief (??)
Q for a Bus (Queue for a Bus)
R for Mo ('alf a Mo)
S for Rantzen (Esther Rantzen)
T for Two (Tea for Two)
U for Me (You for Me)
V for La France (Vive la France)
W for the Winnings (Double you for the Winnings)
X for Breakfast (Eggs for Breakfast)
Y for Husband (Wife or Husband)
Z for Wind (Zephyr Wind)

Two Jigwords using the Cockney Alphabet:

75 | B | O | U | N | C | E |

1. ____ for mutton.
2. ____ for the garden wall.
3. ____ for me.
4. ____ for lope.
5. ____ for miles.
6. ____ for brick.

I 'ave a lot of that.

76 | H | A | T | B | O | X |

1. ____ for bless you.
2. ____ for 'orses.
3. ____ for two.
4. ____ for lamb (for a change).
5. ____ for the wings of a dove (work that one out).
6. ____ for breakfast.

Something to put me 'at into.

CROSSFIT NAMES

```
W W R M A I R I M L J E
I E A E C A R G E A C N
L N L G W E N O N E H I
L D P E U S N E T X A L
O Y H P A M Y T A W R E
U E A D N N E M E O L U
G M N H A D A R D W O Q
H X O H A W D D I E T C
B J E N P N N O J N T A
Y L R R A A J A C K E J
A E L L I J D B R I A N
B R E H P O T S I R H C
```

The word-square above is composed of boys' and girls' names which are written in straight lines, up, down, across, backwards and diagonally. If you cross them out, using the list below, you will find one extra name which is Jigword 77.

DI AL JO REX PAM DAN SUE AMY OWEN
JANE NOEL GWEN JOHN DAWN JACK JILL
BRIAN GRACE RALPH WENDY ANDREW
CHARLOTTE WILLOUGHBY JACQUELINE
BERNADETTE CHRISTOPHER MAX MIRIAM

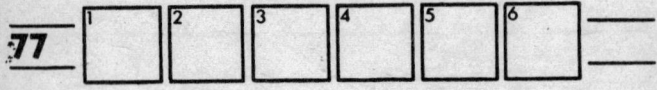

78 | 1 | 2 | 3 | 4 | 5 | 6 |

F I G U R E

Can you work out the Jigword from seeing only the top halves of these letters?

I can't figure that out.

79 | 1 R | 2 M | 3 | 4 | 5 | 6 |

Use the third letter of all the geometric names indicated here:

1. ◯

2. ⊘   semi

3. ⬡

4. △

5. ◇   That's a difficult shape!

6. ◎

Only two of these pictures of Jigg are exactly alike — which two?

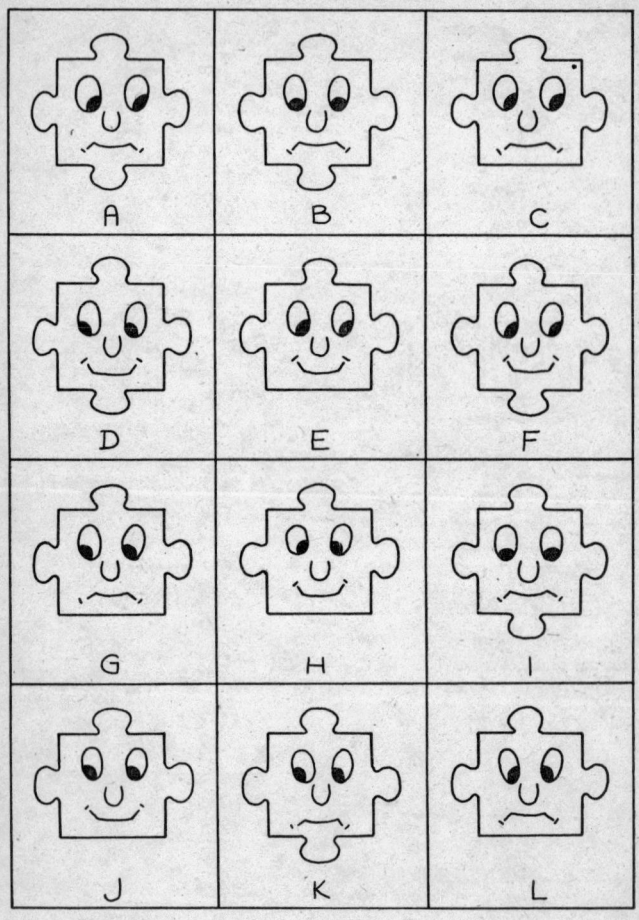

Write down the letters of the two similar pictures.

In only two of these pictures is Adrian wearing the same clothes.

O	P
Q	R
S	T

Write down the letters of the FOUR pictures in which Adrian is wearing different clothes and add them to the letters opposite for a Jigword.

80

1	2	3	4	5	6
	R	O	F	S	T

Whole word clue: Somewhere to eat.

81 [1][2][3][4][5][6] _ _

Here's a very BLACK puzzle.

Use the last letter of each answer.

1. Black as _ _ _ _ (to write with)

2. Black and _ _ _ _ (Irish auxiliary policeman)

3. Black _ _ _ _ _ (not a minicab)

4. Black _ _ _ _ (strike breaker)

5. Black _ _ _ _ _ _ (bubonic plague)

6. Black as _ _ _ _ _ (like a chimney sweep)

Whole word clue: Black _ _ _ _ _ _ _ (on the chess board).

82 [1][2][3][4][5][6] _ _

BCDEFGHIJKNPQRUVWXYZ

Jigword 82 is made from the letters missing from this alphabet.

ROMAN NUMERALS

In Roman numerals letters stand for numbers:

I=1, V=5, X=10, L=50, C=100, D=500, M=1000.

Medieval Roman numerals were used in the Middle Ages, and all the letters but three were used to represent numbers:
I=1, V=5, S=7, X=10, O=11, F=40, A or L=50, S=70, R=80, N=90, C=100, Y=150, T=160, H=200, K or E=250, B=300, P or G=400, A, D or Q=500, M=1000, Z=2000. There are no values for U, W or J.

Friends, Romans and countrymen have a go at this:

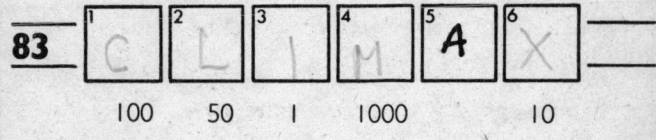

83 | C | L | I | M | A | X
100 | 50 | 1 | 1000 | | 10

And will ye be able to do this one in Medieval numerals?

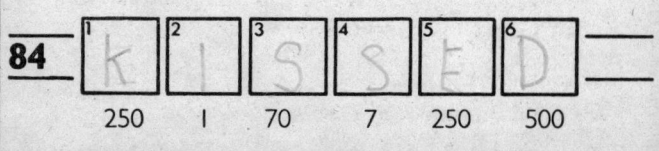

84 | K | I | S | S | E | D
250 | 1 | 70 | 7 | 250 | 500

Here are some more scenes from the last series of my TV programme 'JIGSAW'. I think it's pretty easy to discover the letter each sketch referred to.

85

1. A Mrs Etty Est went to see the doctor. She complained of an it of an ackache and an occasional twinge in her elly. She also had swollen ones in her feet and ruises on her elows. Doctor Artholomew couldn't elieve his ears. Could it e that she was sickening for something, like eri-eri or otulism or uonic plague? No, the doctor diagnosed the prolem without any troule. Mrs Est needed a rain check, for she was utterly rainless, without rain, army, atty, onkers!
She thanked the doctor kindly and wished him ye-ye.

2. A little old ladyl wanted to bluy a little legg plan for bloiling leggs and a ladle. Well, the shlopkleeper had blig ladles and small ladles, slotted sploons, flish slices to scloop leggs out of the plan after they were bloiled. He had legg timers, leggclups and leggsploons as well, but the ladyl really liked the ideal of some leggwarmlers to kleep her leggs warm. Lanyway, the whole lot came to slix plounds slixty-slix plee ... not blad!

3. One way to call the O-men is to do it by mistake. Janet nearly did it when she made up a sentence with only one vowel in it:
'Two poor old fools from London go to Bolton ...'
When Adrian tried the same thing he cheated:
'Lottle Bo Poop, hos lost hor shoop,
Ond dos not know whor to fond thom ...'
       And then he did it!
'... Boo Boo Block shoop, hoov yoo oony wool ...'

OH! dear, in came the O-men.

---

4. Why is it that little boys always ask a lot of questions about the weather?
Why does it rain, Mummy?
Who makes the water vapour, Mummy?
Whose clouds are they, then?
What are clouds thinking about, Mummy?
Where do the water droplets come from?
Which sea loses its water by evaporation to the sky, Mummy?
When does it do that?
Will it come from the sea today?
Whither is it now?
Were the weathermen always wrong when you were a little girl, Mummy?
Wheresover or whether the weathermen will the weather to come, I don't know – but then neither does my Mum!

---

5. Fritz Colditz was an ezcapologizt, who waz practizing ezcaping from a zack when a regiztered letter arrived. Hiz wife Zza-Zza opened it and to their zurprize dizcovered it waz an 'N' (or waz it?).

---

6. The olde blacksmith invented and made a new letter to replace all the 'th's in the olde English writing. When he'd finished inventing he'd come up with a letter that looked like this: Y
His new sign over his shoppe now read:

Yeobald Yatcher
proprietor of   Ye Olde Blacksmiy's Shoppe

Now what do you yink of yat?

THREE MORE NAMES IN REBUS FORM

86

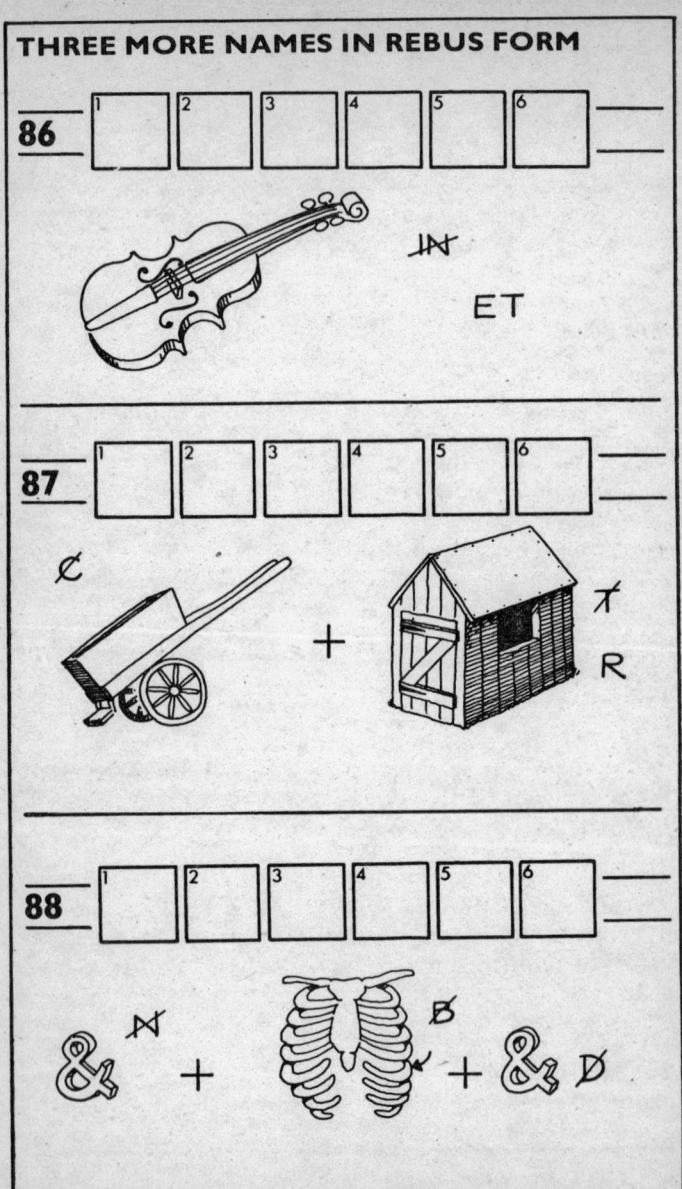

87

88

89 | 1 | 2 | 3 | 4 | 5 | 6 |

Find out the missing letters from these well-known abbreviations:

1. ____.Q.

2. ____.M.C.A.

3. ____.L.O.

4. ____.M.S.

5. ____.E.C.

6. ____.A.A.F.I.

90 | 1 | 2 | 3 | 4 | 5 | 6 |

A different letter is missing from each of these popular TV programme titles. Find out what is absent in each case and you'll find the Jigword.

1. THE GENERTION GME

2. LUE PETER

3. THAT' LIFE

4. NATIONWID

5. THE EWS

6. GRANDSAND

YOUR DRAWINGS
Some letter drawings sent in by viewers

The first six-letter drawings make a word.

The last six-letter drawings make a word too.

Here are a few of your ideas of what you think Biggum looks like above his big Scottish feet.

93

| 1 | 2 | 3 | 4 | 5 | 6 |

TREES
Take the penultimate letter of each answer – that's the next to last letter – and you'll find the Jigword is a type of tree.

1. Where lots of trees are to be found _____
2. The part of the tree in the ground _____
3. The outside of a tree trunk _____
4. The bit of a tree that pricks _____
5. The part that attracts _____
6. Another name for the trunk of a tree _____

94

| 1 | 2 | 3 | 4 | 5 | 6 |

FRUITY
Find the letter which is common to each group of fruits:

1. DAMSON – MANGO – MELON – AVOCADO ____
2. GRAPE – PEAR – PRUNE – RAISIN ____
3. BLACKBERRY – PEACH – APPLE – CURRANT ____
4. CLEMENTINE – GREENGAGE – LEMON – TAMARIND ____
5. AUBERGINE – UGLI – FIG – GUAVA ____
6. STRAWBERRY – CHERRY – LICHEE – OLIVE ____

JANET'S GAME
Here is a picture of a room. On the next page something will be missing. See if you can spot what it is.

SOME CODES

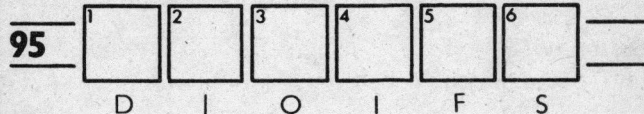

95 ___ D J Q I F S ___

Decode the word by going back one letter in the alphabet.

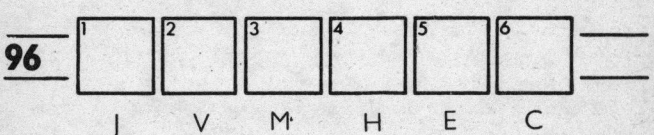

96 ___ J V M H E C ___

The letters of the Jigword have been substituted by others four on in the alphabet.

97 | 1 | 2 | 3 | 4 | 5 | 6 |

BIRDS
First letter of the birds referred to by the clues:

1. Little Jenny   _ _ _ _ _

2. Sacred and scarlet   _ _ _ _ _

3. Songster in the dark? _ _ _ _ _ _ _ _ _ _ _ _

4. Mother and silly!   _ _ _ _ _ _

5. Golden   _ _ _ _ _ _

6. Sign of peace   _ _ _ _ _

OW! OW!
All the words belOW end in OW. Use the first letters for the Jigword.

98 | 1 | 2 | 3 | 4 | 5 | 6 |

1. You can see through it   _ _ _ _ _ OW

2. Spill out of the bath   _ _ _ _ _ _ _ OW

3. Bend over in respect   _ OW

4. The forehead   _ _ _ OW

5. Occupying a position not very far up   _ OW

6. The colour of primroses   _ _ _ _ OW

JANET'S GAME 1

Here is the room again. One thing is missing. Find out what it is and write down its first letter in Jigword 110 on page 79.

99 | 1 | 2 | 3 | 4 | 5 | 6 |

Write down the initial of each of these famous tennis players' Christian names:

1. ____ Borg

2. ____ Ashe

3. ____ Mottram

4. ____ Nastase

5. ____ Goolagong

6. ____ Barker

100 | L | O | C | U | S | T | __

Next to last letter of these:

1. 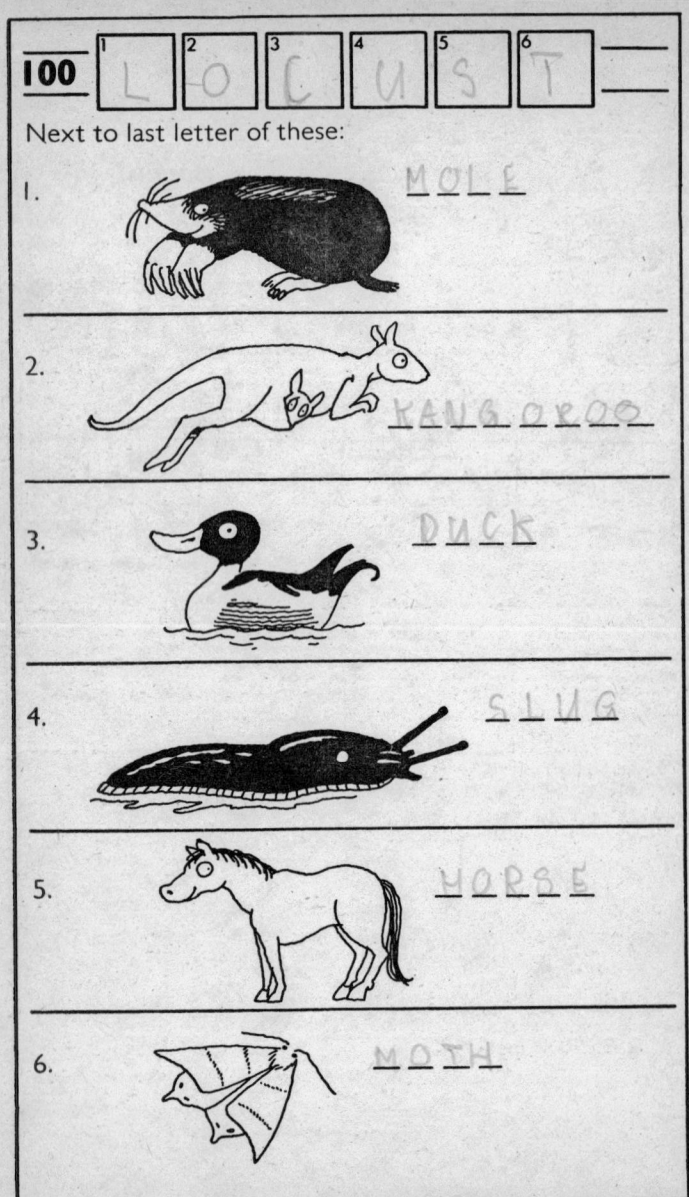 MOLE

2. KANGOROO

3. DUCK

4. SLUG

5. HORSE

6. MOTH

JANET'S GAME 2
Another thing is missing (see page 69).

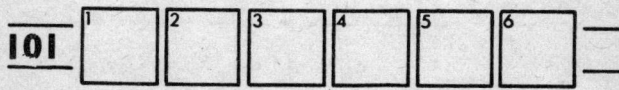

What word do these famous people's Christian names spell out?

1. Sinatra (singer).

2. Pavlova (ballerina).

3. Monroe (film star).

4. Klemperer (conductor).

5. Geller (spoon bender).

6. Kubrick (film director).

And now a very saintly puzzle.

102 | 1 | 2 | 3 | 4 | 5 | 6 | ___

Find out who the Saints are and use the fifth letter of each answer.

1. St _ _ _ _ _ _ _ _ _ _ (shot by arrows).

2. St _ _ _ _ _ _ (West Indian island).

3. St _ _ _ _ _ _ _ _ (of Assissi).

4. St _ _ _ _ _ _ _ _ (London railway station).

5. St _ _ _ _ _ _ _ _ _ (North American waterway).

6. St _ _ _ _ _ _ _ (Smallest city in UK).

JANET'S GAME 3

Write down the first letter of what is missing this time (see page 69).

103 | S | | | | | | __

Use the first letters of the rivers in Europe which answer the clues:

1. The river of Paris.

2. It flows through Rome.

3. The river Bonn is upon.

4. Hamburg is at its mouth.

5. Shakespeare's Stratford is upon it.

6. A light German wine comes from this river's vineyards.

104 | 1 | 2 | 3 | 4 | 5 | 6 | ___

Use the middle letter of each of these:

1. 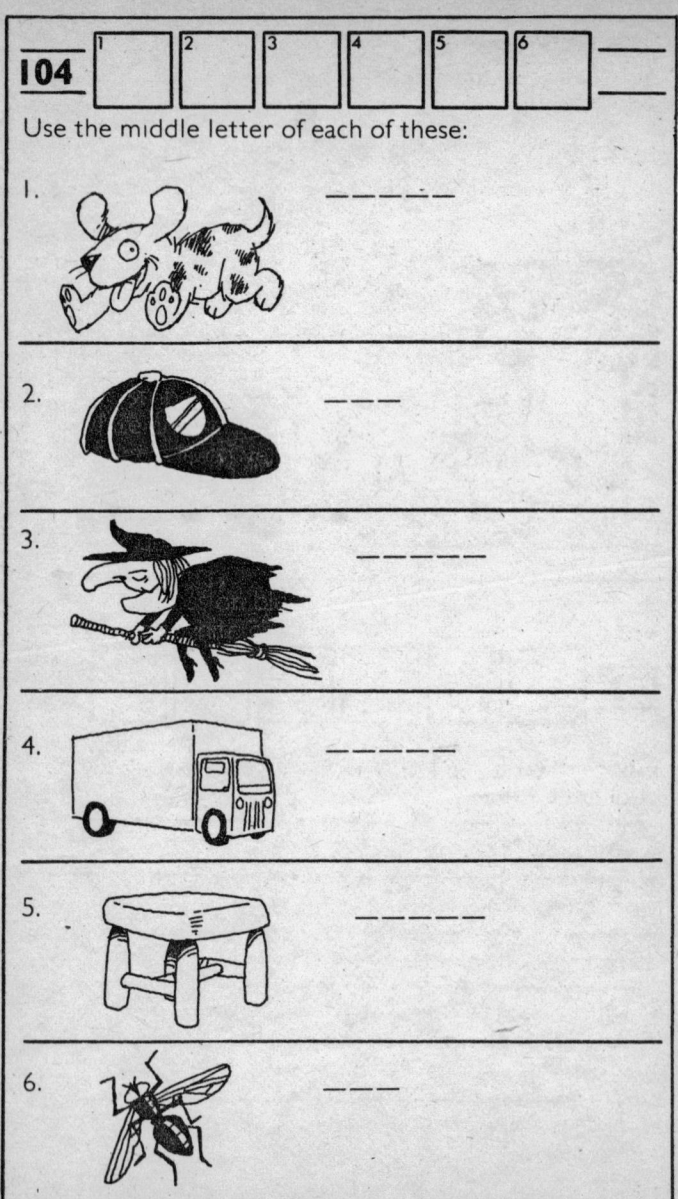 _ _ _ _ _

2. _ _ _ _

3. _ _ _ _ _

4. _ _ _ _ _

5. _ _ _ _ _

6. _ _ _

JANET'S GAME 4
Something else has gone from the room!

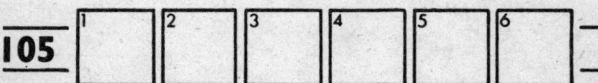

105

Find another country from the first letters of the countries answering the descriptions below:

1. The most 'popular' country in the world.

2. A country on the Adriatic sea.

3. A large West African country.

4. A land-locked country between Pakistan and Iran.

5. Where King Canute came from.

6. The largest island or the smallest continent.

LETTER MAZE

Make your way from the START to the FINISH but only if you can spell out a proper Jigword by going through the right six letters. You can only travel in straight lines from letter to letter.

START

FINISH

106 | 1 | 2 | 3 | 4 | 5 | 6 |

What is the Jigword?

JANET'S GAME 5

This is the fifth thing to disappear, its first letter is the fifth letter of Jigword 110 (see page 79).

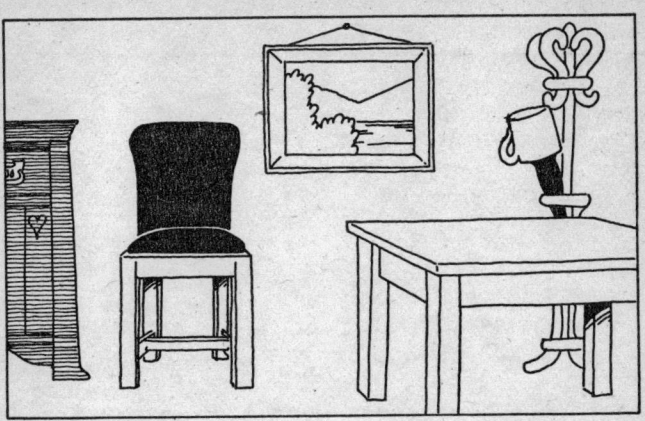

107 | 1 | 2 | 3 | 4 | 5 | 6 |

Some mountains. Use last letters.

1. Highest in England and Wales   Mt____
2. Volcano in Sicily   Mt____
3. Where Noah's ark landed?   Mt____
4. Sacred volcano in Japan   Mt____
5. Highest mountain in Africa   Mt____
6. Sharp-pointed mountain in Switzerland Mt____

CID SLEUTH'S SECRET CODES

Two secret codes where the letters of the alphabet are each represented by a different symbol. The first is called the 'Pigpen Code' and it uses different shapes with and without dots.

A=⌐ B=⊔ C=L D=⌐ E=□ F=⌐ G=⌐
H=⊓ I=⌐ J=·⌐ K=⌐· L=⌐· M=·⌐ N=⌐·
O=⌐· P=·⌐ Q=⌐· R=⌐· S=V T=< U=∧
V=> W=V̇ X=< Y=∧̇ Z=>̇ —

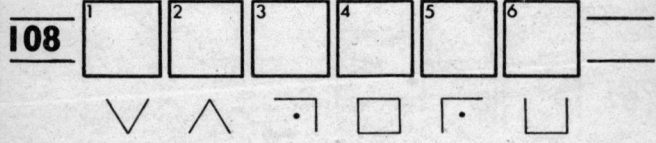

108   ∨ ∧ ⌐· □ ⌐· ⊔

The second secret code is called the 'clock code'. The positions of the hands of a clock represent each of the letters

◷=A ◶=B ◵=C   etc.

This is condensed to:

A=∨ B=∟ C=⌐ D=| E=⌐ F=⌐ G=∨
H=⌐ I=< J=⌐ K=/ L=⌐ M=∨ N=⌐
O=⌐ P=⌐ Q=— R=⌐ S=⌐ T=∧ U=⌐
V=\ W=⌐ X=⌐ Y=⌐ Z=⌐ ·=> END=→

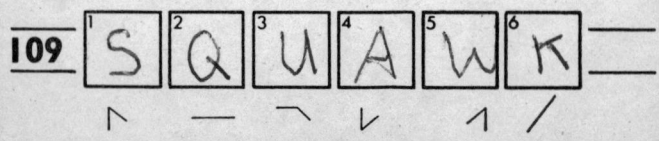

109 S Q U A W K
     ⌐ — ⌐ ∨ ⌐ /

JANET'S GAME 6

Something else has gone — you should have made a word by now, with the initial letters of the things that disappeared.

| 110 | ¹T | ²R | ³U | ⁴A | ⁵N | ⁶T |

The whole word has something to do with going missing.

| 111 | ¹C | ²H | ³U | ⁴M | ⁵P | ⁶S |

Another Jigword is made by the initial letters of all the things left in the room.

INTERNATIONAL CODES

MORSE	SEMA-PHORE	INTERNATIONAL FLAG CODE	
A .—	A	A	White and blue
B —...	B	B	Red
C —.—.	C	C	Blue, red and blue stripes on white
D —..	D	D	Broad blue band on yellow
E .	E	E	Blue above red
F ..—.	F	F	Red diamond on white
G ——.	G	G	Blue stripes on yellow
H	H	H	White and red
I ..	I	I	Black circle on yellow
J .———	J	J	Blue stripes on white
K —.—	K	K	Yellow and blue
L .—..	L	L	Black quarters on yellow
M ——	M	M	White cross on blue
N —.	N	N	Blue and white check
O ———	O	O	Yellow and red
P .——.	P	P	White rectangle on blue
Q ——.—	Q	Q	Yellow
R .—.	R	R	Yellow cross on red
S ...	S	S	Blue rectangle on white
T —	T	T	Red, white & blue
U ..—	U	U	Red quarter on white
V ...—	V	V	Red cross on white
W .——	W	W	Red rectangle in white on blue
X —..—	X	X	Blue cross on white
Y —.——	Y	Y	Red stripes on yellow
Z ——..	Z	Z	Black, yellow, blue & red quarters

Message received

Using the codes opposite, crack these words:

112 WEBBED

113 JACKET

114 SQUIRM

115 FAVOUR

116 LARYNX

(part of your windpipe)

117 PHIZOG

(slang word for your face)

MORE CODES

Two very useful types of codes are braille, used by blind people, and sign language, used by the deaf. Braille appears as little bumps on a flat page so that they can be felt and recognised by fingertip. Sign language is spoken with the hands, and makes visual representation of the letters.

BRAILLE

A B C D E F G H

I J K L M N O P

Q R S T U V W X

Y Z AND CH SH TH

SIGN LANGUAGE

Three letters of the sign language. The complete alphabet can be found in *The Third Book of Jigsaw Puzzles*.

Another very common code, possibly the most widely used, is shorthand; where letters and short words are represented by short dashes of the pen for speedier writing. Here is something written in shorthand:

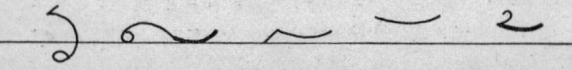

MAP

118 | 1 | 2 | 3 | 4 | 5 | 6 |

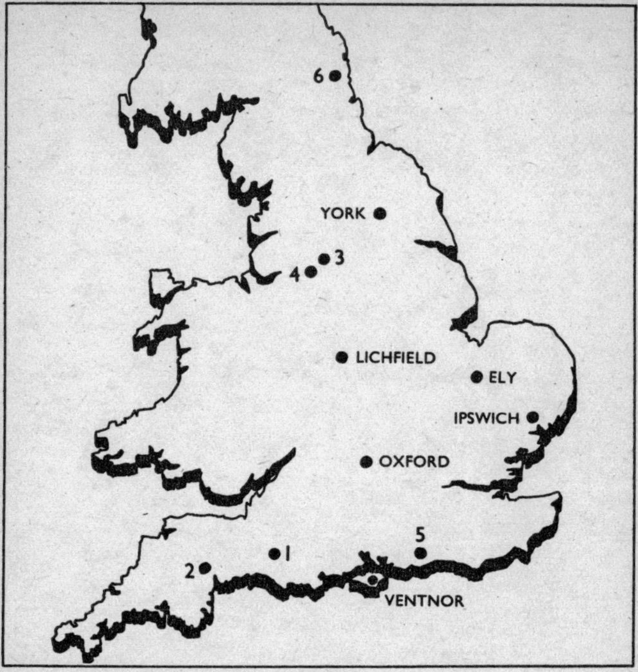

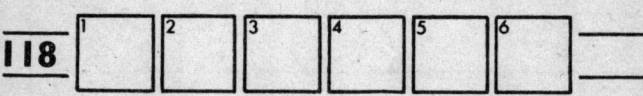

If you write down the towns named on the map, above, in the right order, the name of one of the other towns marked from 1–6 will appear.

119 | 1 | 2 | 3 | 4 | 5 | 6 |

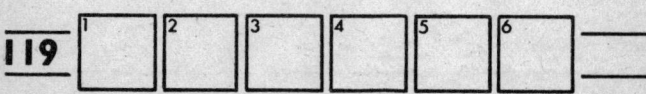

Also the initial letters of the towns numbered 1–6 spell another word – but you will have to look at an atlas for that.

BIGGUM'S JIGSAW PUZZLE NO. 4

How many different-shaped pieces are there in this jigsaw?

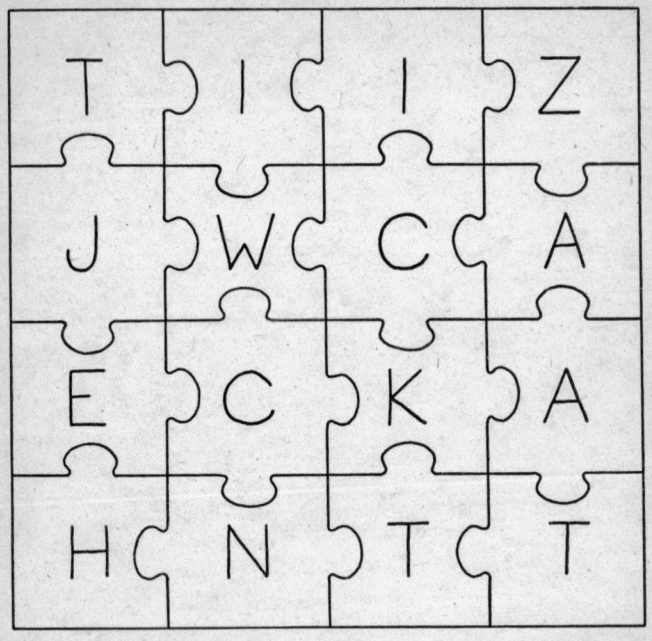

120 | 1 | 2 | 3 | 4 | 5 | 6 |

Take one each of the different shaped pieces, lose one of the letters and make a Jigword. The Jigword is the name of a well-known rugby town in Scotland.

On the next three pages the Jigwords have been split up, not into letters, but into syllables, groups of letters or short words.

121

B	I	S	h	o	P
1	2	3	4	5	6

This one has been split into pairs of letters.

1 & 2. The first two letters mean twice or double.

3 & 4. The second two letters together are a noise one makes to keep others quiet.

5 & 6. The last two letters are an abbreviation for a surgical or military performance.

Whole word clue: You might find him on a chess board.

122

p	a	n	t	r	y
1	2	3	4	5	6

Two three-letter words:

1, 2 & 3. This is a word meaning a broad shallow vessel and it would fit into all these words:

S**PAN**, COM**PAN**Y, UNDER**PAN**TS.

4, 5 & 6. This three-letter word has one meaning which is a score at rugby, and it would also fit in here:

PAS**TRY**, **TRY**ING, EN**TRY**.

123

| 1 | 2 | 3 | 4 | 5 | 6 |

A pair of letters is missing from the front of these words:

1 & 2. __PPER, __NDERGARTEN, __SSING.

2 & 3. __NEY, __NKEY, __NUMENTAL.

4 & 5. __ON, __RWEGIAN, __T.

Whole word clue: You would expect to see a Japanese lady in one.

124

| 1 | 2 | 3 | 4 | 5 | 6 |

Missing words.

1, 2 & 3. Joseph was the ____ of Jacob.

4, 5 & 6. One should use a ____ to catch butterflies.

Whole word clue: A poem of fourteen lines.

125

1, 2 & 3. Find the three-letter word that occurs in all these words:

RANGEFINDER, CURRANT, PRANK.

STRANDED, ORANGE, TYRRANY.

4, 5 & 6. These three letters together stand for the police department which investigates crime.

Whole word clue: Butter is not very nice if it is like this.

126

The two letters occur together in each of these words:

1 & 2. SUPPORTING, TROUPE, BUTTERCUP.

3 & 4. TETRAHEDRON, ROTATION, CORROSIVE.

5 & 6. SPEARMINT, INSULAR, SPARROW.

There are lots more of these type of Jigwords in my Third Puzzle Book and lots of other puzzles, mazes, quizzes and things with Z in them!

ANSWERS

 Here are all the answers

1. SQUEAK
2. POWDER
   Biggum's Jigsaw Puzzle No. 1 – piece E
3. TENNIS (NN = NOON minus O–O)
4. WIZARD
5. VANISH
6. GRUBBY
7. PIMPLE
8. ANGELA
9. SIDNEY
10. VAINLY
11. PARCEL
    Code – Pterry is very brainy and clever. Pterry is a bighead.
12. SICKLY
13. EVELYN
14. MIRROR
15. PIGSTY
16. EIGHTY (egg, ink, gun, hat, toe, yak)
17. NIBBLE (nothing, iron, bra, boot, lobster, eel)
18. BEAUTY (bell, eagle, apple, umbrella, tree, yacht)
19. CORSET (soCCer, rOOt, soRRy, baSS, bEE, neTTle)
20. OXYGEN
21. BOTTOM (riBBon, fOOt, buTTon, raTTle, mOOn, duMMy)
22. CINEMA
23. CASTLE
24. SCORCH
25. MUFFIN
26. UNJUST
27. STIFLE
28. JAMPOT ($22/7 - \pi = 0$)
29. OUTCRY

30. WATERY (shadoW, seA, skirT, sandcastlE, sunbatheR, skY)
    Other 'S' things in the picture:
    sun, shore, seagull, sailing-boat, ship, steam, sand, shell, scooter, surfboard, skin-diver, snorkel, seal, swimmer, shark, spade, submarine, skis, spray, Scotty.
31. SMOOCH (smile, mask, O, O, cape, hair) Other differences:
    buckle, crease in cape, thumb, boot, string, kneecap, P and B, Picture on booth, curtains.
32. BROKEN (booB, pooR, shampoO, cooK, poodlE, MonsooN)
33. CHORAL (sChool, sHoot, fOol, bRoom, lAmpoon, fLoor)
34. RECKON
35. KICKER
36. KIDNAP
37. TIPTOE
38. LAPDOG
39. RUMPUS
40. KITTEN
41. RATHER
42. CATKIN
43. ADDEND
44. GOBLET
45. ARMPIT
46. OFFICE
47. IMPACT
48. PEANUT
49. MAYHEM
50. OUTSET or NITWIT
51. BEDPAN
52. SEESAW
53. NITWIT or OUTSET
54. PIEMAN
55. RUNWAY
56. MIDGET
57. THEBAN
58. OUTFIT
59. SEXPOT

60. LEGEND (walL, gatE, flaG, smokE, suN, fielD)
61. GATHER
62. CHIMED
63. FLAGON
64. ANDREA (AND+REA) [R above REA]
65. BOLTON (BOLT+BONE) [R above, crossed out]
66. FANNIE (FAN+NIE) [N above]
67. CARMEN (CAR+MEN)
68. SHIELD
69. BROKEN
70. TRAMPS
71. DURING
72. FROZEN
73. SPRING
74. THRONG
75. BOUNCE
76. HATBOX
77. DAPHNE
78. FIGURE
79. RATION (ciRcle, diAmeter, ocTagon, trIangle, rhOmbus, riNg)
80. BISTRO
81. KNIGHT (inK, taN, taxI, leG, deatH, sooT)
82. ALMOST
83. CLIMAX
84. KISSED
85. BLOWZY
86. VIOLET (VIOL+ET)
87. ARTHUR (ART+HUR)
88. ADRIAN (AD+RI+AN)
89. HYPHEN
90. ABSENT
91. EXPORT
92. MAKEUP
93. SORREL (foreSt, roOt, baRk, thoRn, flowEr, boLe)
94. ORANGE
95. CIPHER
96. FRIDAY
97. WINGED (wren, ibis, nightingale, goose, eagle, dove)

98. WOBBLY (wIndow, overflOw, Bow, Brow, Low, Yellow)
99. BABIES (Bjorn, Arthur, Buster, Ilie, Evonne, Sue)
100. LOCUST (moLe, kangarOo, duCk, slUg, horSe, moTh)
101. FAMOUS (Frank, Anna, Marilyn, Otto, Uri, Stanley)
102. SACRED (SebaStian, LuciA, FranCis, PancRas, LawrEnce, DaviDs)
103. STREAM (Seine, Tiber, Rhine, Elbe, Avon, Moselle)
104. PATROL (puPpy, cAp, wiTch, loRry, stOol, fLy)
105. CANADA (China, Albania, Nigeria, Afghanistan, Denmark, Australia)
106. VOYAGE
107. NATION (SnowdoN, EtnA, AraraT, FujI, KilmanjarO, MatterhorN)
108. SUPERB
109. SQUAWK
110. TRUANT (tablecloth, rug, upholstery, armchair, newspaper, table)
111. CHUMPS (chair, hatstand, umbrella, mug, picture, sideboard)
112. WEBBED
113. JACKET
114. SQUIRM
115. FAVOUR
116. LARYNX
117. PHIZOG
118. YEOVIL (York, Ely, Oxford, Ventnor, Ipswich, Lichfield)
119. YEOMAN (1. Yeovil, 2. Exeter, 3. Oldham, 4. Manchester, 5. Arundel, 6. Newcastle)
120. HAWICK
121. BISHOP (Bi – Sh! – Op)
122. PANTRY (PAN – TRY)
123. KIMONO (KI – MO – NO)
124. SONNET (SON – NET)
125. RANCID (RAN – C.I.D.)
126. UPROAR (UP – RO – AR)

Clive Doig would like to thank the following for their help in the preparation of this book:
Sheila Elkin, Malcolm Bird, Jeremy Beadle, Joan Doig, Jitka Martin and Richard Simkin. The poem in Jigword 61 clue 5 was written by Chris Emmett and clue 5 Jigword 85 was based on a sketch written by Peter Campbell.

The drawings on pages 62 to 65 were submitted by Emma Barrett, Lorraine Bristow, Heather Collins, E. Emery, A. Harris, Christine Hillyar, R. Van Homan, Darren Humphreys, Steven Jones, Amanda Marsh, Sara Pawley, Heather Pead, Linsey Yorke Pheasant, Maggie St. Rose, Michelle Shaw, Kulvinder Virdee, Mark Warner and Andrew Wishart.

Here are a few blank pages for you to make up your own Jigwords and Clever Clues.